Under the California Sun

Under the California Sun

*One Man's Journey Through
Life, Family, and Culture*

by

Ernesto Montellano Salazar, Jr.

RISING RIVER BOOKS
Olympia, WA
2023

Under the California Sun
One Man's Journey Through Life, Family, and Culture
© 2023 Ernesto Montellano Salazar, Jr.

All rights reserved. No part of this publication may be reproduced or utilized in any form or by any means, electronic or mechanical, including photocopying, recording, or by any information storage and retrieval system, without permission in writing from the publishers. The information contained herein is for interest only and does not constitute medical advice.

Book & cover design by Jenn Zahrt.
Cover photo by Jessica Christian.

Publisher's Cataloging-in-Publication
(Provided by Cassidy Cataloguing Services, Inc.).

Names: Montellano Salazar, Ernesto, author.
Title: Under the California sun : one man's journey through life, family, and culture / by Ernesto Montellano Salazar, Jr.
Description: Olympia WA : Rising River Books, 2023.
Identifiers: ISBN: 978-1-947544-99-4 (paperback)
Subjects: LCSH: Montellano Salazar, Ernesto. | Racially mixed people--California--Biography. | Indians of North America--California--Biography. | United States. Army--Officials and employees--Biography. | LCGFT: Autobiographies.
Classification: LCC: E184.A1 M66 2023 | DDC: 305.8009794--dc23

ISBN: 978-1-947544-99-4
Printed worldwide through Ingram.

Rising River Books
A Revelore® IMPRINT
1910 4th AVE E PMB141
Olympia WA 98506
United States
www.risingriverbooks.com
First printed in 2023.

to my wonderful family

Contents

Foreword: Explorations of Voice — 9
by Jeff M. Salazar

Introduction: Composing Your Life Story & — 13
How I Would Like to Be Remembered

Chapter 1: I'm From a Time in the 40's	16
Chapter 2: First Ten, the Early Years	19
Chapter 3: The Person I Most Admire	22
Chapter 4: The Patriarch of My Family	24
Chapter 5: My Mother's Family	26
Chapter 6: The Montellano Side of the Family	31
Chapter 7: I Am From a Human Wrecking Yard	37
Chapter 8: The One Room Schoolhouse	39
Chapter 9: Radio and Television	42
Chapter 10: Music in My Life	45
Chapter 11: What I Did as My Summer Vacation	48
Chapter 12: Where Someone Loves Us Best of All	50
Chapter 13: My Life in the Military	53
Chapter 14: Ultimatum	57
Chapter 15: A Burden on Your Shoulder	60
Chapter 16: The Advice in My Life	63
Chapter 17: Unfinished Business	65
Chapter 18: My Head in the Clouds	68
Chapter 19: Cars	71
Chapter 20: Family Heirloom	74
Chapter 21: What Was I Thinking?	76
Chapter 22: Children, Then and Now	79
Chapter 23: Reunions	82
Chapter 24: Tools	84

Chapter 25: That's Not How I Remember It	87
Chapter 26: When a Door Opens and Lets the Future In	90
Chapter 27: Animals I Have Known	93
Chapter 28: Influenced By	96
Chapter 29: Famous Last Words (You're Not Going to Make It)	99
Chapter 30: What Do You Want to Be When You Grow Up?	102
Chapter 31: A Year of Aging	105
Chapter 32: Where Would You Like to Go This Year? Who Would You Like to Go With?	108
Chapter 33: Road Scholar	110
Chapter 34: What Was I Thinking?	115
Afterword: From Sierras to Salazar and Beyond by Jeff M. Salazar	117

Foreword
Explorations of Voice

IT BEGINS WITH A MYSTERY...how did my family get the name Salazar? All our family records show that we come from Juan Tomás Sierras and Dolores Estrada (Salazar), and yet, I grew up not knowing much beyond my Grandfather—and even that knowledge was but an arm's distance away from his truth.

Ernesto Montellano Salazar, Jr., my grandfather, is a mountain of a man—steadfast, strong, secure. As the beloved patriarch of my family, Grandpa Ernie has always been an almost mythical figure. I have always looked up to him. What I didn't realize is that this very mythic status obscured my ability to see him and his life in brilliant, real detail. So, I wrote him a letter asking him deep questions about his life. I tried to get him to share things only he would know and that only he could express. He wrote back, and his answers were everything

I'd hoped for. They illuminated hidden parts of his life and showcased a true American experience, namely, an Indigenous American experience.

He navigated a landscape riddled with pitfalls and pleasures: as a sole provider raising an extended family at an extremely young age; as a serviceman in the Armed Forces following World War II; as an avid car lover and recreational pilot. Reading about his life from his Indigenous American perspective gives us an unrivaled glimpse of our nation's attributes, both good and bad, and, for that reason alone, it is a story that needs to be preserved and shared. I encouraged him to write all his stories down in a journal. I was sure the rest of the family would love to read it, and he thought it was a good idea. But as we continued our weekly phone calls and letters, we never talked about it again.

Five years later, in early 2022, he and grandma Kathy drove up from San Luis Obispo to my home in central Washington State. He came to the front door with a binder in his hand and a smile on his face. He had enrolled in a writing course at their local community college. Each weekly assignment was based on life experiences—stories from early childhood, reflections on children, how they planned on spending summer—things like that. All his writings, notes, and assignments were there in the binder with a heap of pictures. I was blown away.

He had carefully documented his own experiences throughout his life. As he relives the past, he courageously shares the difficult parts alongside the easy-to-relay good memories. Always careful to reflect his own perspective, he is honorable in his responsibility and owning his agency over the decisions he's made. His is an ordinary life, but in that ordinary life there is greatness and inspiration. In the afterword, I provide more ancestral backstory and further contextualize the life and the times of this Indigenous American.

And so, I invite you to share the story of my grandfather, *Ernesto Montellano Salazar Jr.*

Jeff Salazar
Olympia, WA
July 2023

Introduction
Composing Your Life Story & How I Would Like to Be Remembered

I NEVER THOUGHT THERE WAS ANY VALUE in my life story. I feel like a very average person with average experiences. My grandson Jeff encouraged me to compose my life story for my family. I never thought of it myself. I have four children, nine grandchildren, and four great-grandchildren. Besides California, they are scattered all over the country in Washington, Texas, Oregon, and Kentucky.

I was lucky to find this class so convenient in Arroyo Grande where I live. I felt very inadequate in my writing skills. With a great teacher in Russ and the good people in this class, I am encouraged in a very non-judgmental way. I'm glad I have stuck it out. I get good feedback from my classmates and apply it to my stories. I feel it improves my writing.

I find the subjects that we are assigned each week are helpful. When I go about my writing, I think of how the subject applies to my life. I then sit down to put it on paper and the stories just flow.

As I reach the autumn of my life, I wonder how I will be remembered. I didn't live a remarkable life, although it was a well lived life. I tried to leave more friends than enemies. I cared what people thought of me as I went through that journey.

To my work colleagues, I hope to be remembered as an employee who was loyal to the company that gave me a paycheck. I got along well with my co-workers and I valued those who worked for me when I became a supervisor. I left PG&E with a good reputation.

To my children, I would like to be remembered as a good provider and a good father figure. I don't think I had all the answers but I tried! They could always get a hug from Dad, and they still do. Three out of four ain't bad.

My oldest son and I are estranged, although he got the same love and discipline as the others. I guess I failed him, and I regret it. I always considered myself a "work in progress" as a parent.

To my neighbors and my community, I would like to be remembered as a good worker. I have always been a volunteer in the community and have volunteered for the Food Bank for 19 years. I try to be friendly with my neighbors and keep a nice yard so the neighborhood looks good.

To my wife, who is the most important person in my life, I hope I was her best friend. She is my best friend and helps me be a better person.

Lastly, I would like to be remembered by everyone else that I have met as a decent person who treated them with respect.

Ernie Salazar
November 15, 2017

Chapter 1
I'm From a Time in the 40's

I STILL REMEMBER THE LA OF MY YOUTH. The air was clear and we could see the San Gabriel Mountains every day. Traffic was not a problem because not all families owned a car. Gasoline was rationed during the war and your allotment was determined by your job importance. We used public transportation which was very efficient. I learned how to use it by the time I was 8 years old.

My parents both worked during the week so I became very independent at an early age. I could fix my own breakfast (usually corn flakes) and walk to school by myself. When I came home from school, I changed out of my school clothes and looked for my friends so we could play. We played marbles, spun tops, played war games or Cowboys and Indians. We would play outside until my parents came home from work. They hollered for me to come wash up when dinner was ready. I can still remember the smell of my Mother making tortillas. She would make them fresh for every meal and wouldn't keep them for the next meal if any were left over.

My Mother's only brother Frank was drafted not long after Pearl Harbor and trained as any Army Medic. He saw action from the invasion that started in Italy and ended in Germany.

My Uncle Frank sent home two boxes of souvenirs while over there. I became popular in my neighborhood because I had those items to share with my friends who like to look at them.

A few months after we received those items, we received a smaller box. My parents were not home yet so I quickly opened the box that I assumed was from my Uncle Frank. I looked at the contents and thought he had sent me a dead German. My Aunt had actually sent my Mother some beef jerky and some other products. I didn't bother to read the return address and simply tore the wrapping off the box. I told my friends it was a dead German and they were lined up outside our apartment to see him. When my Mother got home, she sent all of the kids home. She looked at the contents of the box and saw that my Aunt had sent her beef jerky. I never lived that one down!

My Uncle Frank returned home safe but was suffering from PTSD. It wasn't recognized as a problem at that time and returning Vets weren't being treated for it. My Uncle died in his mid 40's from cirrhosis of the liver caused by the alcohol he consumed.

Everyone supported the war effort without complaining. I had two other Uncles that were killed in action and were Gold Star Veterans. I look back with admiration for all of the sacrifices that were made. It was the best of times and the worst of times. I was there and I learned how to be independent as a result.

Chapter 2
First Ten, the Early Years

My first memories start around 1939 when I was four years old. We lived in Glendale, California. My Father Ernest, Mother Alexandra, Grandmother Dolores and I all lived together in a small two bedroom home which was common in that era. My father wanted my Grandmother to live with us. He always supported her and treated her like gold. My Mother was very fond of her and they got along very well. In those years, it was the norm to have several generations living together.

I liked my Grandmother very much because she took me everywhere she went. She way very light complected with white hair and green eyes. She was a Mayo Indian from the Northern part of Mexico. She was born in 1878 and died in 1942.

It was very windy one week in Southern California. One of my first memories was of a large tree falling on our house while my Grandmother was taking care of me. We were not injured but it scared us.

We had other relatives in the neighborhood and visited with all of them often. They were all related to my Grandmother.

I also remember when Pearl Harbor was bombed. All of my older cousins were listening to the radio and they all knew they would soon be fighting in Europe or the Pacific. I remember how everyone was in shock.

I had started school and soon realized the value of being bilingual. We had segregated classrooms, which was the norm, but the kids that spoke only Spanish were punished and were considered slow or retarded. They were put in different classrooms. I am thankful to my parents for thinking ahead and protecting me.

When my Grandmother died in 1942, we had her wake in our living room. This was also the norm. After that, my Father was restless soul. We moved often and he could find work easily during the war. I went to several schools and it was hard making new friends. I was a loner and I hated being put in that position. I applied myself in school. I was not a great student, but I passed anyway.

We moved from Los Angeles to San Jose where my Grandfather Juan and my Step-Grandmother Josefina lived with seven of their eleven children still at home. My Uncle Frank, my Mother's brother, was also part of the equation at that time. He always worked and paid his way until he went to war. My Father could not serve because of a heat stroke he had suffered when he was 26 years old.

We moved back to Los Angeles, then back to San Jose. In 1945, when I was 10 years old, my parents separated and my Mother went back to Los Angeles where her family lived.

My parents gave me the choice of living in Los Angeles with my Mother or San Jose with my Father. My Mother always worked and I would be by myself if I went to Los Angeles or I would be part of a big family if I stayed with my Father in San Jose. I chose San Jose and was part of my Grandfather's family while my Father continued with his itinerant ways. I am grateful that my parents always put me first.

As I reached my 10th year in 1945, WWII ended which changed the world.

Chapter 3
The Person I Most Admire

MY GRANDMOTHER HAS ALWAYS BEEN MY hero. She suffered many hardships but always had a smile on her face. She believed that God would provide and get us through any problem.

My parents divorced in 1945. My Mother moved back to Los Angeles and wanted me to go with her, but I didn't want to go. My Grandmother invited me to stay with my Grandfather and her. They still had seven of my Dad's Half-brothers and Sisters at home, but she made room for one more.

My Grandfather had cancer and was getting frail. My Dad always sent her money and my Uncles and I worked in the fields to help out. We gave every penny we made to Grandma. Grandpa died in 1947 and we moved to the country. The house we lived in had no electricity, running water or inside plumbing. We chopped wood for the stove, filled kerosine lamps and carried water into the house. At night we played cards, Monopoly and told stories under the kerosine lamp. Grandma would pray for us every day.

We brought vegetables home from the fields and after it rained Grandma would walk the fields to gather mushrooms and swiss chard. She knew which mushrooms to pick and none of us got sick! She bought a sack of flour, a sack of pinto beans and a sack of potatoes for the month. We always had enough to eat and never felt like we were poor. We were thankful for what we had and we were happy. She had a beautiful smile and always offered to make coffee and feed anyone who came to visit. She believed in sharing whatever she had and always made you feel welcome.

She had a hard life but never complained. She lived into her 90's and the world was a better place because of her!

Chapter 4
The Patriarch of My Family

HE WAS A TOUGH INDIVIDUAL. He had to be to survive at the end of the 19th century in the Arizona Territory. My ancestors came from that area, and he was my Grandfather. He was born in 1887, and died in 1946 of cancer. Juan Sierra was his name and he wore it proudly. He was six feet tall and handsome like a Cary Cooper character. He worked as a miner or vaquero (cowboy) to make a living.

My Grandfather was an excellent horseman. He worked for the Vickers and Vail Empire Ranch in Southern Arizona, which was one of the biggest cattle ranches in the west. My Father was his oldest son, but he didn't meet his Father until he was 15 years old. I guess it was common in those days.

My Grandfather was sent to herd cattle on Santa Rosa Island off the coast of Santa Barbara in the early 1900's after the owners of the Empire Ranch bought the island in 1902. They sold it to the US Government in 1987 for $29 million! While on the island, my Grandfather married the woman who ran the kitchen, and they had four children. I don't know what happened to that marriage, the first marriage, or if they were married at all, but my Grandfather returned to Arizona and married his third wife. They moved to Los Angeles, where he worked as an extra in Western movies because of his cowboy skills. However, he couldn't make enough money to support his family. The Depression affected everyone in the country, and our family was no exception. My Grandparents followed the crops to the Santa Clara Valley. The family worked in the fields and eventually the canneries.

I remember Grandpa as a kind and gentle man. He would always tell stories and folklore. He was great with us kids.

In Arizona they have an annual celebration at the Empire Ranch, and they encourage family members of the vaqueros to attend. The Ranch is now a historical site and is maintained by a non-profit foundation. Some of my family who live in the area attend frequently. My family was able to attend in 2013 and had a great time. We were treated very well and encouraged to share our memories of my Grandfather. We plan to return again in the near future.

Chapter 5
My Mother's Family

SHE WAS NOT A COMPLAINER. She excepted life as it came and I now understand why she was such an introvert.

She was born in 1917, the oldest of four children. Her father was a copper miner near the border of Agua Prieta, Mexico (Dark Water) and Douglas, Arizona. It was a rough life for the whole family. Her father and his brother were caught in a mine cave-in. Her father lost a leg and his brother lost his life. He then bought a little neighborhood store and eked out a living for his family. Her mother was not in very good health. My mother had to cook, clean the house and watch her younger siblings. My grandfather died young and his wife followed soon afterwards.

My mother's aunt, who lived in Bisbee, Arizona, took the two oldest children, my mother and her brother Frank. The two youngest sisters were sent to an orphanage and my mother lost track of them. My mother's aunt treated both children like indentured servants. As good fortune sometimes happens, another aunt and cousin came to visit from Los Angeles. They did not like the way the kids were being treated and asked to take them with them to Los Angeles. The aunt that had taken them originally gladly gave them up. My mother's Los Angeles relatives were much more welcoming. They treated them better and gave them a better life.

My mother and her brother were enrolled in school. They finished Junior High School and did not continue. There was a lot of discrimination at the time, something I also experienced as I was growing up. I am not sure how my parents met, but I believe it was while working in agriculture. They married in San Jose, California in 1934. I came along in 1935 and was born in Glendale, California. My father was digging ditches for a plumbing contractor when we lived in Glendale. He was always working and was proud of his work ethic. Unfortunately, he had a heat stroke at the age of 28 that slowed him down a bit.

My mother would always talk about her sisters who were left behind in Mexico and wonder what had become of them. Being an undocumented person, she didn't pursue looking for them. My father then got involved!

I remember taking the train with my father to Douglas, Arizona when I was about 6 or 7 years old. I enjoyed the ride. The trains were crowded with soldiers and sailors during the war. We arrived and checked into a hotel in Douglas. The next day we crossed the border and went to the Government building to find some information about my mother's sisters. Being bilingual sure helped. We got the information we wanted.

One sister, Otilia, was adopted by a poor family. The youngest sister, Clementina, was adopted by an upper middle class family and was sent to get a good education. Somehow the two sisters had met and kept in contact.

My father found what he had come for. I met both my aunts. My aunt Otilia had two children, a little girl named Consuelo and a boy named Fernando. My cousin Consuelo would have a big impact in my life although I didn't know it at the time. My mother was overjoyed with the news. She worked at a candy factory and saved enough money to have the two sisters travel to Los Angeles on a Visitor's Visa. They never lost track of each other again.

As the years went by, family dynamics changed. My wife, three boys and I traveled to Mexico to see them a couple of times over the years and kept in contact. Tragedy impacted the life of my cousin Consuelo. Her husband had drowned while swimming in a river, leaving her with four boys and an infant girl.

My cousin Fernando asked my wife and me to be the best man and matron of honor at his wedding in Mexico. We accepted. We attended the wedding and were planning to return home the next day. My cousin Consuelo asked if we would take the infant girl home with us. Mexico is a Third World Country and life was hard. My cousin was forced to leave her four boys locked in her small house while she worked 12 hours to make enough to feed her brood. She was going to give the baby away if we didn't take her home with us. My first wife Carmen and I had three sons and she always wanted a girl. It sound like god had sent this little girl to us, but I wasn't going to break the law by taking the baby home with us! We extended our stay by two days and went to the US Consulate in Mexicali, Mexico to see how to bring her back with us legally. We were told we would need to fill out several forms to apply to bring her back and talk to the man in charge. We waited five hours for him, but he never came to work that day. I made a decision to see the US Consulate in San Francisco where I had more resources. I also needed to get back to work. I crossed the border with the baby and headed for San Jose. I knew the way!

Bad luck was our reward for breaking the law. Two days after we got home the baby stopped breathing and turned blue. My wife rushed her to the hospital. When I got there from work, she was in an oxygen tent and a priest was giving her last rites. God must have been in the tent with her because she survived with no brain damage. I called my attorney from the hospital and he said "you did what?" He advised me to go to the Consulate in San Francisco to declare her and hire an attorney in Mexico to work from that end. After many trips to San Francisco and Mexico dealing with bureaucrats on both sides of the border, I received help from a Veteran's group and Senator Allen Cranston. My daughter finally got legal status at the age of 13. She is the light of my life. She has three children and is a Social Services Supervisor for the County of Santa Clara. I am the the only father she has known.

My mother, her siblings, Consuelo and Fernando have all passed on. I feel fortunate to still have part of my mother's family in my life. In addition to my daughter, I have a half sister Pat who lives in Santa Maria.

Chapter 6
The Montellano Side of the Family

I DON'T KNOW TOO MUCH ABOUT my maternal Grandparents or that side of the family. My Mother Alexandra was the oldest of four children. She had two sisters, Otilia and Clementina, and a brother Frank Jr. My Grandfather Francisco worked as a copper miner in Cananea, Sonora, Mexico, along with his Brother. They worked deep underground and were caught in a cave-in. My Grandfather lost his leg and his Brother lost his life in the accident.

Using a small pension and a modest saving account, Grandpa Frank purchased a building and established a neighborhood grocery store which allowed him to eke out a living.

My Grandfather and his wife Teresa Cordova suffered from poor health and died young leaving their four children orphans. As it is customary in our culture, relatives would step up and take in the orphaned children when possible. One Aunt who had no children took my Mother and my Uncle. My Mother was 8 years old at the time and my Uncle was 6 years old. The two younger sisters were sent to an orphanage.

My Mother and Uncle Frank were taken to Bisbee, Arizona to live with their Aunt. They were not treated well. The Aunt only took them in to work for her cleaning house, doing other chores and treated them like indentured slaves. They lived in Bisbee for 5 years.

Other family members came to visit from Los Angeles. Aunt Louisa was a very generous and compassionate woman. When she saw that the children were not being treated well, she offered to take them to Los Angeles to live with her. The Aunt from Bisbee was glad to give them away.

Thus, a new chapter began in my Mother's life. She and my Uncle Frank were enrolled in school and treated very well. My Mother applied herself in school and was fluent in both English and Spanish.

Her new family would work in agriculture as migrant farm worker during the summer. While working in the fields, she met my Dad Ernest who was also working in the fields as a migrant farm worker with his family. They fell in love and married in the summer of 1934. They moved to Glendale, California, where I was born in 1935 and my Uncle Frank came to live with us.

My Dad worked as a laborer for the Butterfield Plumbing Company. He dug ditches to lay sewer pipe and worked very hard to support his family. He suffered a heat stroke at work in 1937. After recovering, he had a limp and partial paralysis, but kept working. No one had health insurance or worker's compensation in those days. It was a much simpler time and we somehow managed.

My Mother never forgot about her two younger sister and always wondered what had happened to them.

As the second half of the 1930s passed, we still felt the remnants of the Great Depression. War was looming in Europe and Asia.

The attack on Pearl Harbor on December 7, 1941, impacted every family in the country. We saw a large number of our young men go off to defend us. I was 6 years old at the time and remember how proud my Uncle and Cousins were as they went off to war. Unfortunately, they were treated as second class citizens. My Uncle Frank was drafted in the early 1940's and saw some of the most difficult battles in Europe. He served about four years and came home with no apparent physical injuries. However, he returned home with many psychological problems that were never treated.

He died in his early 40's. I still consider him my hero for all he saw and experienced. My Dad was not able to serve because of his heat stroke, thank God!

Around 1943, my Dad decided to go to Mexico to see if he could find my Mother's two sisters and took me with him. My Mother was not able to go because she was undocumented and was afraid to go anywhere near the border.

We traveled by train to Douglas, Arizona, and met many nice and respectful servicemen on the train. Once in Douglas, we stayed at a hotel and crossed the border to Agua Prieta (dark waters.) We went to the Hall of Justice to check their documents and records. We discovered both sisters were adopted. Otilia, the oldest child, was adopted by a poor family and Clementina was adopted by a middle class family. We found both women and were surprised to learn that they knew each other. They were delighted to meet us and learn about their two older siblings. The siblings began communicating soon after. My Dad made a lot of points with everyone for his efforts.

Otilia, the oldest of the two sisters, had two children at the time. She had a son named Fernando and a daughter named Consuelo would later have a big impact on my life. Clementine never married and was afflicted with arthritis as a young woman. She was a very studious and religious woman.

Otilia and Clementina came to visit my Mother in Los Angeles on a tourist visa. It was a great reunion for all of them. As the years passed, they kept in touch with our family.

After I married and served my time in the military, I visited them in Mexicali, Mexico on several occasions. We sent money and took them clothes. When Otilia's son Fernando got married, my wife and I were their matron of honor and best man. It was a nice occasion, but shortly thereafter my Cousin Consuelo's husband drowned while swimming in a river. She was left with 5 children - four boys and an infant girl.

As a widow, my Cousin Consuelo had to work to support the children. She couldn't stay home to take care of the baby girl, so she asked if we would take her child to raise. My wife Carmen agreed to take the child and she was able to stay in the family. I was reluctant at first but agreed to do it if we could do it legally. I went to the American Consulate in Mexicali and spent two days trying to get permission to bring the baby to the United States. After running into many obstacles that I couldn't overcome, I bought her new clothes, brought the infant home and decided to work from my side of the border. I hired a lawyer in San Jose and one in Mexicali, went to the Immigration Department in San Francisco and Tijuana, and tried to resolve her status. With the help of the CSO Organization, The American GI Forum and the office of Senator Alan Cranston, I finally obtained her green card after 13 years of meeting obstacle after obstacle. She later became an American citizen as an Adult. My daughter Maria is very special to our family and is worth all the effort and money. And, I think she likes her Dad!

My Cousin Consuelo and her four boys became legal immigrants and moved to San Jose, California. My Aunt Otilia followed shortly thereafter with her second husband Jesus and her third child Aurora. My Mother got to spend time with her sister and family as we all lived in San Jose at the time. Fernando and his wife stayed in Mexico as did my Aunt Clementine.

Most of the family has passed away by now, including Consuelo in 1997. I am thankful, though, for the time we were able to spend together as a reunited family and will always be grateful to Consuelo for her gift of my daughter.

Chapter 7
I Am From a Human Wrecking Yard

IN A WRECKING YARD, THE LUSTER that once was is gone, replaced by rust and a faded facade. The streamlines that were once admired are outdated and archaic. The strong roar of the horsepower engine is now silent. The engine is just considered a gas hog with leaks and smoke. A once recognizable fresh look is now a scratched up body that is waiting for the scrap heap.

The human condition is the same and it comes with age. You walk slower. You don't hear as well and your conversations are not longer stimulating. Most of your friends are gone. Physical limitations hinder the projects that you want to do.

The golden years suck. All you have left are the memories of years past, but I am glad I still have that.

I have seem dramatic changes in society. Instead of making life better, technology and the internet makes it easier for someone to rob you. Now even your banker is not trustworthy!

I am lucky to have lived my life as it was, but I worry about the world I am leaving behind for my grandchildren and their children.

Chapter 8
The One Room Schoolhouse

WHEN MY GRANDFATHER PASSED AWAY, I was living with my grandparents. Because we were dirt poor, we moved from town to the foothills of Milpitas where rent was cheap. My dad helped as much as he could to support my grandmother, his brothers, his sisters and me. The house was old and drafty but it was a roof over our heads. We all knew how to adapt to our environment.

We had no inside plumbing or running water and used a wood burning stove for heat. We chopped wood and carried water. We used kerosene lamps at night.

Grandmother Josephine took us to a school called Air Point for the next semester. This was in 1947. It was a one room schoolhouse that had one teacher, Mrs. Viola Tompkins. She taught grades 1through 8. There were about 15 students from the surrounding area. She was about 60 years old with poor vision but was a very dedicated teacher with a difficult job. I look back with nothing but admiration for her. She was fair with everyone and didn't have favorites.

We had a clean environment that was a source of pride for us. We cleaned the chalkboards and floors before we went home. The grounds were sparse but had some playground equipment. There was no inside plumbing at school either.

We seemed to have plenty of school supplies. When the weather was bad

there was a potbelly stove to keep us warm. We also had a Victrola that she played. When we couldn't go outside, she made us dance and sing songs.

We really walked to school since there was no bus service. It was about 2 miles each way. Mrs. Tompkins drove a La Salle coupe and we would watch her park in the carport. Many times she would knock some boards loose because of her poor vision.

She spent as much time with each student as she could to make them succeed. When she was working with the students in one grade, the rest of us would be working on our assignments or homework.

Mrs. Tompkins taught at Air Point School for many years. Teachers seemed to be valued more then they are today, or maybe I am being unfair in my opinions. I had a great time attending that one room schoolhouse and I think I benefited from the experience.

A county park and Golf course now stand where the schoolhouse use to be. The building was demolished years ago and only memories remain for the students that Mrs. Tompkins taught.

Chapter 9
Radio and Television

AROUND OUR HOUSE, Saturday was my favorite day. My Mother would buzz around dressed in a house dress with an apron over it. She was ready to seize the day and catch up on her chores for the week.

The radio was our entertainment. I would listen to "Let's Pretend" while I had my cornflakes. My Mother would then listen to "Grand Central Station" while she did her housework. She would sing along with songs from "Hit Parade." My Mother washed clothes in a tub with a washboard while she sang her favorite songs. She had a very nice voice.

I would go look for my friends to play stickball or marbles. We would hope the Helms Bakery truck or the ice cream truck would come by. The ice deliveryman would come by also and we would hop in the back while he was delivering ice blocks to look for ice chunks. We owned an ice box like most people.

My Mother had a light with an added plug hanging down from the ceiling in the kitchen. When she was ironing she would sometimes add another appliance and blow the fuse. My Father would fix it by adding a copper penny to get us by until he bought more fuses. We were lucky he didn't burn the house down by overloading the circuit.

My Father would listen to Walter Cronkite for news about the war. My Father could not pass the draft physical because he had suffered a heat stroke in 1938. During the war families hung small flags in the window with stars on them. Each blue star was for a family member serving in the war and a gold star was for a serviceman who was killed in action. Our family flags hanging in the window had many blue stars and even a few gold stars.

We listened to FDR's "Fireside Chats" and Joe Louis fights on the radio. Our favorite programs were "Gang Busters," "The Shadow," and "Fibber McGee and Molly."

We would go to the movies and shopping in downtown LA. It was very nice and safe then. All of the stores were there since there weren't malls in the suburbs at that time. We would take the Streetcar to get around because gasoline was rationed. Your allotment was determined by your job importance.

We had a nice Zenith radio that my Father has bought for us. We were entertained and happy with it. I didn't own a television until I got out of the Army in 1955 after serving in the Korean War. My first television was a used RCA with a 13 inch screen that looked a lot like our console radio.

Chapter 10
Music in My Life

MUSIC HAS PLAYED A BIG PART IN MY LIFE. I call it my drug of choice. Music reminds me of certain years of my life, people, places I have lived or the artist that performs it. My Mother, Alejandra, use to sing as long as I can remember and she had a good voice. I don't remember when she started encouraging me to sing along with her. We knew all of the old standards and anything that was popular at the time. We would always listen to the "Hit Parade" on the radio. That radio program was the one in the 40's!

Being a bi-lingual family, we also knew the Spanish music standards. I think music made us happy no matter what language.

My Father, Ernesto, couldn't carry a tune. My Mother said it was because of the heat stroke he suffered in 1938, but he still enjoyed listening to the Spanish programs and music.

In the Hispanic culture, music is the center of many celebrations such as weddings, baptisms, birthdays, anniversaries, quinceaneras, and even some funerals. Liquor was also a big part of the festivities. The old customs die hard, but are changing. In the last few years, most of the family reunions I have attended have been alcohol free and I agree with that concept.

In my early teen years, I developed a love for the blues. I listened to the Black Radio Stations from Oakland and San Francisco. I also listened to Contemporary Latin Music from Cuba, Puerto Rico and New York in the late 40's and early 50's. Another place I went to enjoy music was the Majestic Ballroom on First Street in downtown San Jose. It was the "hot spot" on Saturday night to meet girls and dance to Latin music. I missed very few of these dances.

I always listen to music on the car radio and attend concerts with groups that I like. One of my favorite things to do is go to Concerts in the Park on Sundays. I am lucky that my wife Kathy also enjoys concerts and we do like the same type of music. She isn't quite as big a music fan and her horse events always take priority - different strokes for different folks!

Growing up we always had guitars laying around. One of my Uncles showed me how to play a few basic chords on the guitar. I also passed that along to my sons. They became more proficient than I was and performed in various bands during the 60's and 70's.

I remained only good enough to play on the porch, but I am happy playing for myself. I have a tremor in my right hand so my guitar playing is diminishing, but I still try! Music will remain in my life as long as I can still turn the knobs on the radio, put CDs in the CD player or carry a folding chair to our local Concerts in the Park.

Chapter 11
What I Did as My Summer Vacation

SUMMERS IN THE EARLY 1940'S were not an enjoyable time for me! It meant a time to work in the fields to help your family. There were no child labor laws that applied to anyone so kids worked. It was a time to save for school clothes and other essentials that your family counted on.

In the summer we went to the Santa Clara Valley to pick cherries, apricots, pears, walnuts and prunes. We also met other families and played in the evenings when we weren't working. I don't know where we got all the energy. For Thanksgiving week we would travel to the San Joaquin Valley to pick cotton, my least favorite week off.

During World War II everyone worked to help the war effort since all able-bodied men were off to war. Women stepped up and filled the void. My Father had suffered a heat stroke in 1939 and was declared 4F, not eligible for the draft. Around 1943 my parents changed from agricultural workers to industrial workers, but I still worked in the fields with my Grandmother and Cousins until I was 13 years old. It was an easy transition for them since both my parents were bilingual and English was our first language. My Father was a hard worker and could always find a job. His words of wisdom to me were to work harder than your peers and they will keep you longer.

I feel fortunate to have lived during those years. Everyone sacrificed but our country was united, more than I ever remember it being.

Chapter 12
Where Someone Loves Us Best of All

WHEN I WAS A YOUNG MAN OF 15 YEARS, my Father trusted my judgement and would leave me alone for days. I tried to make good decisions so I could keep that trust, but sometimes I failed.

I had two friends that I hung out with who were schoolmates and lived in the neighborhood. The came from big families and I was a lone wolf who lived with one parent.

One weekend my friend George got into a heated argument with his parents. He and Lee, my other friend, decided to run away and wanted me to join them. I didn't have any problems at home, but I thought I would go with them. They came to our apartment with a plan. They thought we should catch a freight train going south and I thought it sounded like fun.

I grabbed three cans of food from our house so everyone could take a can along. Since it was spring, I didn't expect cold nights and I only took a windbreaker. We went to the railroad yard and found a train moving slow enough to jump on. We settled in an empty boxcar and discovered the door would not close. We forgot to bring a flashlight which wasn't good planning on our part. We took turns staying awake. After several hours we made it to the Salinas Valley and the train stopped for quite a while. We were hungry and shared a can of Spam. We wanted to get off to gather some vegetables, but they were quite a distance away. We were afraid to get left behind or separated so we didn't get off the train. It was very cold and windy.

We talked to a couple of hobos who were much better equipped for that type of travel. They laughed at us but wished us well. The train finally started moving and we were on our way again. I was tired of our trip and wanted to go back. I even considered hitchhiking, but George convinced me to keep going.

We continued on our trip cold and hungry. While George and I slept, Lee ate our second can of food. He ate the Pork and Beans all by himself without sharing with us. I felt like pushing him off the train!

We arrived in San Luis Obispo and the railroad cops caught us. I thought they might give us passage back to San Jose. But, after pushing us around, they put us into another boxcar on a train going north.

The ordeal wasn't over yet! All we had left to eat was one can of corn which we shared. We slept a lot and tried to stay warm. After the third day we arrived back in San Jose hungry, cold and dirty.

My Father was home when I arrived and was glad to see me. I took a long, hot bath and ate everything I could find.

We laughed about it later, settled our minor grievances and they made up with their families. We were finally back where someone loves us best of all!

Chapter 13
My Life in the Military

IT WAS A NICE SPRING DAY in the Santa Clara Valley in April, 1953. I went to get the mail after the mailman drove away. I had been a member of the National Guard for about a year and a half and was expecting my monthly check. Instead, I had a letter from the Draft Board informing me I was being drafted into the Army on May 8th. I had missed two National Guard meetings and they turned my name into the Draft Board.

I reported as requested and boarded a bus to the Induction Center in San Francisco. The first day was mostly administrative and included physical exams. We were then bused to Ford Ord in Monterey County. The next morning we were issued uniforms, other gear, given many shots and got our hair cut short. The following morning some of us were bused to Camp Roberts in San Luis Obispo County for 16 weeks of Basic Training.

My best friend, George Smith, was also drafted since we had both missed our National Guard meetings. He was also sent to Camp Roberts so I had company.

The first day of basic training was memorable. George and I were assigned to the 4th Platoon. Since we both had prior experience, George became the Platoon Leader and I became a Squad Leader.

Our company was made up of men from all walks of life and parts of the country. Our First Sargent was named Jim Wilcox and he was a seasoned veteran. He had just returned from combat in Korea, was in top physical condition and challenged anyone of us to a fist fight if we thought we could whip him. No one challenged him. He looked like Clint Eastwood and was built just like him. We all admired him and found him tough but fair.

It had been only five years since President Truman had integrated the Military and some people were still not happy about it. There were soldiers that came from the Deep South where segregation was the law. We learned to co-exist because our First Sargent demanded it.

Half way through our Basic Training, the truce was signed with Korea and we all celebrated the news. We completed our training and waited for our orders.

I was ordered to Germany where there was a shortage of soldiers to patrol the Iron Curtain. I was made a tank driver when I arrived in Germany. It was October and the weather was cold and damp. The country still had many bombed buildings, but they were rebuilding and restoring the damage 8 years after the end of WWII. We were the Occupation Troops and were there to keep the Russians at bay. My Battalion was stationed in Landshut, Germany, 60 km north of Munich. The people were nice but they didn't want to talk about the war so I respected their wishes.

We were in the field most of the time and I saw a lot of Bavaria in Southern Germany. We also spent every third month patrolling the Czech Border and the Russian zone of Austria.

I didn't enjoy their winters, but I was able to travel to Holland and Denmark on my own. The people were courteous and interesting. I tried to be a good example of our country.

Most of my fellow soldiers were from the East Coast and the South. They had a lot stronger opinions on segregation than a California Native like me. I made friends easily with most of them because I didn't take sides. I completed my required 18 months of Active Duty and I am proud to have served my country.

My best friend George Smith was stationed in Alabama. He, unfortunately, was in a bad car accident and ended up in a wheelchair for the remainder of his life. We remained good friends until his death in 1993.

I have been fortunate enough to travel to Europe three times and have enjoyed it each time I have gone back. Both my wife Kathy and I love Europe.

Lately, though, I feel like I have been living in a time warp for 64 years. Our country is dealing with a lot of the same issues we faced when I was in the Army. We are still at odds with Russia, are still in Korea with North Korea threatening war again, and our country is still struggling with integration issues. We don't seemed to have learned from History or found lasting solutions to age old problems.

Chapter 14
Ultimatum

I FIND THIS THEME MORE DIFFICULT to write about than other subjects. I guess I associate ultimatums with conflict. I always tried to understand the ground rules and abide by them. This goes back to my upbringing. I tried to find out how to co-exist with my peers and live by my "Dad's Rules" even when I disagreed with some of them. The most important ones were to just get along and show respect.

As a young man I wasn't a pushover. I boxed as a teen and I fought my way growing up on the poor side of town. But, that was a different time. I would get into fights because bullying was alive and well even then. Whether you won or lost a fight, you dusted yourself off, shook the other guy's hand, and then walked away. These days people resolve conflicts with a gun or a knife.

I regret dropping out of High School. In the 50's there was plenty of work. My priorities were girls and cars. I was old enough to know better but young enough not to care. My first ultimatum was subtle but there just the same. I told my father I was dropping out of school and his comment was "Well, son, stop by and see me sometime. If you are not going to school you have to fend for yourself." I was surprised at his ultimatum, but he meant what he said. I had to plan what to do. I had worked the summer in the cannery and bought my first car, so I could sleep in it if I had to. I rented a room in a roominghouse and a found a job in construction. It was hard work but the pay was good. What the hell was I thinking? I regretted not staying in school. I learned to do things on my own, but school was more fun.

Two years later I was drafted into the Army. I didn't deal with ultimatums there, we just followed orders and did what we were told.

I was working at PG&E and was offered a job as a supervisor. I was reluctant about taking the job. As a journeyman machinist, I was only responsible for the work I did. As a supervisor you are not only responsible for the job you are assigned but are also responsible for different personalities of the people who work for you and the work they perform. I had worked for different bosses and I learned what was right and what was wrong. In my day it was "My way or the highway." I did take the supervisor's job and had guidelines to help me be a good leader. We had employee evaluations every six months. If you had performance problems, that is where you dealt with them. If the problem continued after two documented warnings, the employee was given a paid day off to think about his job as part of the third evaluation. He was given an ultimatum and had counselors to talk to if he needed one. During refueling outages the company brought in temporary contractors from all over the country. They were given work expectations but I still had clashes with a few of them and had to fire some. The company was great to work for and the people at DCPP were talented and professional. Luckily, I didn't have to give too many ultimatums!

Chapter 15
A Burden on Your Shoulder

I WAS DRAFTED INTO THE ARMY IN MAY 1953 for missing three meeting while I was a member of the National Guard. We all knew the consequences for missing meetings during a war situation so I brought it on myself. I was from the wrong side of the tracks and my dad taught me how to handle myself.

I had a girl at the time and we were going steady. While I was on leave, she told me that her mother was suffering from kidney problems. She was concerned that she might lose control of her kids if she got worse. The father was long gone by then, and my girl Carmen was the oldest at 17. She wanted to get married so she could take care of her brothers and sisters if her mother got sicker. I was shipping out overseas and thought it was the noble thing to do, although it might not have been the smartest decision.

When I returned from overseas I left the military.

We settled into civilian life, lived close to her family and started our own family.

In 1960 my mother-in-law's illness got worse, She asked to talk to me in private. On her deathbed she begged me to watch over her family and not let them go to an orphanage. It was a profound moment in my life. I was 25 and had three kids of my own to support. But, how could I possibly refuse a dying women her last request? How was I going to shoulder that responsibility? My grandmother would always say if you do the right thing God will help you.

My mother-in-law died in the summer of 1960. I took in my Wife's two brothers and two sisters. We owned a three bedroom house and had to use bunk beds so we could all fit. I had lived like that also when I was growing up and I was use to living with a lot of people in a small home. I worked two jobs to make ends meet. There was always food on the table and our bills were paid. In the summer my wife and her siblings worked in the fields to make money for school clothes. All of them graduated from high school and one went to college. Now that we are all adults, they tell me how grateful they are that we helped them. When they ask if I have any regrets, I tell them I would do the same thing again if necessary.

I kept my promise to a dying person and I don't regret it. I guess my grandmother's advice was true.

My first marriage lasted 23 years and didn't end well. I have, however, been able to maintain a good relationship with my in-laws. Two of them call me on Father's Day and Christmas and we always have a good time when we are able to get together. I never dwell on what I didn't have, but am thankful for what I did have.

Chapter 16
The Advice in My Life

MY FAVORITE ADVICE IS that you have three choices in life: you can lead, follow or get the hell out of the way.

My Father advised me to treat others the way you would like to be treated, and I passed that wisdom along to my children. Respect others, and they will show you respect. Think of what you are going to say before you say it, since you can't "unring a bell."

I don't like to say I am sorry and that I didn't mean it. I say what I mean, or I don't say anything.

My parents advised me to apply myself in school and it would help me succeed. School in 1951 was not that easy for me. I had a Social Studies teacher that advised me to drop out of school and help my family since I would not finish high school anyway. Even though I was a B student, his remarks influenced me, and I dropped out of high school.

After I dropped out, I worked in construction for two years. I was drafted into the Army and spent another two years patrolling the "Iron Curtain Border" during the Korean War. When I returned from the service, I went back to school, got my high school diploma, and completed two years of community college. I worked as a machinist and tool and die maker for General Electric in San Jose.

I was then offered a job with PG&E for more money as a traveling machinist and relocated to the central coast. I retired as a maintenance supervisor, and I considered myself successful in my line of work.

I guess I felt put down by my teacher, but he motivated me to rise above his advice and show him I could do it. We didn't have role models with college degrees at that time. Anyone with a steady job was considered successful. I feel I achieved the American Dream. I also feel fortunate to have grown up during the Depression and World War II. Life was simpler and people were more honest, even politicians. If you worked hard as you were advised, you could find a job, buy a house, and send your kids to college.

Chapter 17
Unfinished Business

YOUR LIFE STORY DEPENDS A LOT ON the choices you make, whether good or bad. There are also circumstances beyond your control that you have to maneuver through. Most of my life I've had good examples that I could follow, and I tried to be a good example for the people who depended on me. I had more luck than brains.

My first wife Carmen had a harder time dealing with family problems than I did. As the oldest in a single parent family, she was the one who set the example for her siblings. She lived through harder situations than I did.

It was all new to me. As an only child, I felt lonely growing up. Being around other families made me happy. Being a father figure was a challenge for me, and I wanted to be successful at it. She, on the other hand, had assumed a parent role by helping her mother all of her life.

When her mother died and left her three siblings for us to raise, she felt the burden more than me. My job was to be a provider outside of the home. She filled the homemaker role very well for several years.

Carmen was a little overweight and was self conscious about it. It never bothered me in any way. She started working as a nurse to help us financially. She asked the doctor for a prescription for diet pills. I guess it curbed her appetite and gave her energy.

I use to pay the bills and handle other expensives. I knew what doctor bills were coming in and I started seeing bills from other doctors for the same prescriptions. There were also prescriptions for anti-depressants. She started sleeping more than normal. I asked her why and she didn't want to talk about it.

She had two suicide attempts. I asked if she wanted to end our marriage and told her that taking her own life was not worth it. After the second attempt she said she needed to get away for a while. She went to stay with my best friend and his wife in Long Beach.

She found other friends and finally wore out her welcome with my friends. She would come home occasionally. I did my best to keep things together for the kids while still working. I finally gave her a choice or ultimatum. We could stay married or file for divorce.

She chose the latter.

It was an ugly divorce, but it was better for both of us. My daughter was the only minor still at home and she took it the hardest. She was given the choice of living with her mother or me, and she chose her mother. She lived in bad neighborhoods. She later decided she would have been better off if she had lived with me.

Carmen continued with the drugs and her friends. She eventually ran out of friends and her health. She died in 1994.

I started going out with Kathy, my present wife who also worked for GE. We married in 1979, and I consider myself very lucky to have her in my life. We have been married for 38 happy years. When one door closes in your life, another door opens. I lucked out. All of my kids love her, and she is grandma to all the grandkids and great-grandkids.

Although my first wife Carmen's health deteriorated with drugs, I don't like to put her down to my children. It was a dark time in my life, but I don't dwell on those dark days. I try to be grateful with my life.

I don't want to make Carmen the villain. If I had it all to do over, maybe I shouldn't have worked as many hours and been away from home so much. I'll accept some of that blame.

Chapter 18
My Head in the Clouds

As a child I was always fascinated with airplanes. I dreamed of getting in an airplane some day and going for a ride. In the early 1940's it was only an impossible dream, especially considering my circumstances. I was poor, a minority and no one I knew had ever gone up as a passenger.

As a child growing up during WWII, I fantasized about being a fighter pilot and shooting down enemy planes. I could identify many of the WWII planes and those pilots were my heroes. But, reality prevailed and planted my feet on the ground again!

While in the military, I traveled many miles and many oceans as a passenger. I enjoyed the experience most of the time.

In the 1970's, I worked for GE in San Jose. One of the mechanics who worked for the company, Hal Osbourne, asked if I had ever had a ride in a small airplane. I said "No, but I would like to go for a ride."

We met at the airport and I was hooked! My head was in the clouds. I was working with Hal and told him about my childhood dreams. He was a Certified Flight Instructor and asked if I wanted to take flying lessons. I told him I couldn't afford it even though I didn't know anything about the lessons or the cost. I was raising a family and they came first. He knew I loved airplanes, so he explained I could get my pilot's license for less than $1,000 which included lessons and practice time. I was sold!

Hal was a great instructor. He was very skilled and disciplined so I got my money's worth. When I solo'd, it was the most exhilarating feeling of my life. I fulfilled my childhood dream and accomplished what was impossible, or so I thought! I eventually qualified to fly seven different single engine planes. I flew all over the western United States and Mexico. I continued to fly until I had heart problems and couldn't pass the FAA physical to maintain my license.

When I lived in the Bay Area, I volunteered for an organization called the Flying Doctors as a pilot and interpreter. Being bilingual was a definite help. They hooked me up with a Dentist from Palo Alto and I helped him fly his six passenger Cessna 210. We flew to remote areas in Mexico to proved free medical care. Movas in Sonora, Mexico was as remote an area as the group serviced. The landing strip was short with a dirt runway. I went with the dentist twice without problems.

On November 11, 1979, I had agreed to go on another trip with the Flying Doctors. However, due to a death in the family, my wife's grandmother, I had to cancel. The plane crashed in Mexico with five people on board. The 6th seat was mine and was empty. Attending the funeral saved my life, I almost bought the farm.

When we moved to the Central Coast for my new job, I tapered off my flying. Although I still have my license, my health keeps me from piloting an airplane. Last year I was able to check another item off my bucket list by taking a ride in a biplane. I fulfilled one of my life long dreams of being a pilot and I cherish the time I flew with friends and family.

Chapter 19
Cars

I STILL LOOK BACK IN TIME and think about the impact cars have had on my life. I was fortunate to live in the era of great cars that were all made in the United States of America. You could look at a car and identify its year and make. Although I believe cars are better and more reliable now then in the past, they all look the same. You now have to go to the dealer or a technician to have your car repaired because they are full of computer chips and plastic. However, they are more reliable and run longer.

I learned to drive at 14 years of age. I worked at a dairy and drove a truck to feed the cows and handle hay bales. My Uncle Percy taught me how to drive, how to work on vehicles and how to troubleshoot problems.

I got my driver license in 1952. After working all summer at the canneries in San Jose, I bought my first car—a 1941 Chevy Club Coupe. It was metallic green with beige upholstery. If you had one of the better cars you were more popular with the girls. Those were my "American Graffiti" days. We would cruise the Main Street in San Jose and hit the drive-in hamburger joints when we had used the gasoline that we had. Gas was cheap then at 25 cents per gallon. Drive-in theaters were also popular and the girls like them too. I drove that Chevy until I was drafted for the Korean War when I gave it to my Mother's only brother Frank.

After two years in the Army driving a tank, I was discharged and married my first wife. I bought a 1949 Mercury which was a great, fast car. Three years later I bought a beautiful 1956 Chevy Bel-Air hard top, but it had an electrical problem. I traded it for a 1957 Chevy Bel-Air which I kept until 1969. I then bought a 1962 Cadillac which was very nice and reliable. It had beautiful lines and subtle caddie fins.

I eventually bought a new 1969 Chevy Pickup with a slide-in camper. By then I had to grow up and think of my wife and three boys. We started visiting National Parks in the United States and Canada. There wasn't any grass growing out of my truck tires, no sir! We covered all of California and the Pacific Northwest in that pickup.

My wife started working and I bought her a new 1972 Chevy Chevelle. When we divorced in 1976, I kept the pickup and she kept the Chevelle.

After moving to the Central Coast, I bought a 1985 Chevy El Camino in Arroyo Grande. I kept the car for about 30 years and put almost 300,000 miles on it. During that time I put in a new engine and transmission. I gave it to my grandson who is in the Air Force. He drove it from California to South Carolina and then to San Antonio, Texas when he was transferred. He tells me it won't be long before he hits 500,000 miles. We take care of our cars and have them serviced as recommended. He also keeps it garaged. Our agreement is that he will give it back to me if he tires of it. My second son has a 1969 Chevy Camaro that is is completely restored and very valuable.

I hope we can keep these cars in the family, even after I'm gone.

Chapter 20
Family Heirloom

SOMETHING OF VALUE IS AN ITEM that you treasure and that reminds family members of you when they see it. In September of 1985, I purchased a brand new 1985 Chevrolet El Camino. Being a car guy, I always liked the El Camino. It became an old friend and all of my family and friends identified the El Camino with me.

It was a two-tone grey with a cab high camper shell. I always took care of my vehicles and kept them in the garage. My wife Kathy and I drove it to Vancouver, Canada, in 1986 to the World's Fair. We also drove it all over the West Coast and I drove it to work every day for over 20 years. I took meticulous care of that vehicle and drove it until it had 277,358 miles.

I eventually gave it to my grandson Michael who is in the Air Force. However, there were conditions with the gift. First, the El Camino was not to be sold. If he no longer wanted it, he was to be give it back to me or to his father, my son Sonny. It was to be kept in the family. Second, it was not to be modified but was to be kept as original as possible.

Michael drove it from California to South Carolina and is currently stationed in San Antonio, Texas. It now has 497,218 miles on it and still runs great. The El Camino is one year older than Michael. He keeps it garaged at his home also.

Sonny and I are going to visit Michael, his wife Melissa, and their two children Hayden and Anthony next month. I am planning on driving my old El Camino around Texas and fulfilling another item on my bucket list. Although it will probably be a rougher ride than my Honda, I am looking forward to driving it. Over the years I have driven a wide range of vehicles such as a Model T Ford, a Model A Ford, an 18-wheel semi-truck and a Volkswagen Bug. I have never lost my love of cars and it will be a treat for me to drive my old friend again.

My grandson Michael always liked old cars, and I am happy he treasures my old El Camino too.

Chapter 21
What Was I Thinking?

WE WERE VISITING MY IN-LAWS in Arroyo Grande during Christmas in 1980. As usual it was a beautiful December day on the Central Coast. My wife was raised in Arroyo Grande and always liked going home.

At the time both my wife and I worked for the General Electric Motor Plant in San Jose. My wife was the purchasing manager and I was a tool and die maker. We were both happy in our jobs.

We had previously seen an advertisement in the San Jose newspaper for Machinists at PG&E's Diablo Canyon Nuclear Power Plant. I didn't pay much attention to the ad since my wife and I both had good jobs at General Electric. I had been with the company for sixteen years.

My wife suggested that I submit a resume and see if they would respond. I submitted my resume but didn't expect them to respond and forgot about it. To my surprise, I was called and asked to come in for an interview and to take a test while we were visiting my In-laws. Curiosity got the best of me, so I went for the interview and took the test. I really wasn't serious but wanted to test my interview skills. PG&E said they contact me with the results.

As luck would have it, they offered me a job! What was I thinking? I was raised in the Santa Clara Valley, had family there and I liked my job. I told my closest friends at work and they said I was crazy. My wife left the decision up to me, but she liked the idea of going home to live.

I pondered my decision and couldn't sleep. I don't make snap decisions like that and change is hard for me. I had to respond to the job offer, though. The money and benefits were better than I currently had. I told my boss and he said he hated to lose me. He also told me that once I made my decision, never look back and always look forward.

San Jose was growing by leaps and bounds. The traffic was horrible and getting worse. I asked myself "Do I want to live and retire here or do I want to move to the Central Coast?"

I made my decision and quit General Electric.

At first I didn't like my new job. It required a lot less skills than my previous job but was more diverse. Learning made up for what I thought was my loss of skills. The people were great, but I was homesick and missed my family. What the hell was I thinking?

In the end, the move turned out for the best. Three years after I left General Electric closed the Motor Plant and moved the operations to New York state. I had a good career at PG&E. I retired as a Maintenance Supervisor and was brought back to work the outages until 2015. And, I love the area where I retired!

Chapter 22
Children, Then and Now

As someone once said, children come into the world without a manual. You learn as you go through life every day. Your value system, taught to you by your parents and grandparents, is your guide. You do the best you can with what you have. I raised seven kids. My first wife and I had three boys and one girl. My three in-laws came to live with us after my mother-in-law died. My first wife Carmen and I started having children in the 1950's. We were married for 23 years. We were happy and committed for the first 18 years of marriage.

I have to give her credit for being a good wife and mother in those early years. I worked long hours at two jobs for many years. I always tried to make myself available to all of them, including my three in-laws. We were involved in Cub Scouts, Little League Baseball and paper routes. It was always a team effort. If they got into trouble, they were sent to their rooms as punishment.

They were not allowed to watch tv or listen to the radio, but they had books they could read and a guitar that was given to me by a friend. I could play the guitar and I taught them all the basic chords. I guess I banished them so many times they became good guitar players. As they grew into their teen years, they formed a garage band. Other kids that liked music started coming to our house. I was not thrilled because my grocery bill was getting bigger, but I always knew where they were.

My in-laws were no trouble either except one of the boys who was dyslexic. We were unaware of this condition. We would scold him for being lazy and he was put in a slow-learner class. I failed him.

I use to talk to them about higher learning and I feel like I failed at that, too. I always thought that life began when the dog dies and the kids left home but I was sad when that happened. My marriage came apart about the same time in 1977. After we were divorced, she became addicted to diet pills and god knows what else.

As for my relationship with all of the children, it is good with six out of the seven. My oldest son moved to Montana and I don't have much contact with him. I get cards and phone calls from the rest.

My two sons that live in California still play in bands, so my form of punishment paid off for them. My three in-laws moved out of state, two to Colorado and one to Arizona. We keep in contact and visit occasionally.

I have nine grandchildren and four great-grandchildren. Even though they didn't go to college, they always worked, made a good living and were able to support their families. I use to fix things for them, but now I find myself asking them to fix things for me. I feel blessed and lucky to have good kids.

Chapter 23
Reunions

The last family reunion I attended was two summers ago. It was held at Alum Rock Park in San Jose. It included a catered luncheon but no alcohol was allowed. It was well attended by about eighty people, and the weather was nice. The reunion was for my grandfather's side of the family.

My grandmother's side of the family all live in Southern California. I don't have as much contact with them, since I seldom travel there.

We were encouraged to bring old family pictures of relatives to share. As I am one of the older family members, I had quite a few pictures and stories to share. Everyone was very respectful and nice. The younger ones played organized games. The older ones played cards or sat around and talked.

The generations have changed over the years. When I was growing up you were very close to your relatives.

Our whole structure was to visit aunts, uncles and the elders of the family. I knew all of my cousins . We shared special occasions like religious holidays and celebrations, weddings, baptisms and funerals. Quite a few of the present generation only see each other at these reunions and some were meeting for the first time.

After visiting with the majority of the people, my wife and I sat down with my cousin Eleazar. He assembled our family ancestry book in the early 1990's using copies of census records plus catholic and government documents including birth certificates, marriage licenses and death certificates. Since he did all of the research himself, he is a wealth of information.

At the reunion we had a special guest, a cousin we had never met. He had more information to add to our ancestry book which he had gathered from his parent's and grandparent's experiences. This information was added to our family history as a supplement document.

We try to have a reunion at least every five years. We come away with new memories that have been shared and can be added to our family history. We all seem to leave more energized, excited to catch up with one another and learn a little more about the family that binds us together.

Chapter 24
Tools

I have always been fascinated by tools. I guess it began when I was about 7 or 8 years old and got a Lincoln Log Set for Christmas.

In those dasy you only got one gift. I was skeptical about Santa Claus because we never had a house with a chimney that he could climb down. I always wanted an Erector Set, but was happy with my Lincoln Log Set. I would spend hours building things instead of playing with Log Cabin Syrup containers and my collection of Brillantine Hair Oil Bottles. I would later build a scooter and a car out of 2x4's, orange crates and other available materials. The key was finding wheels or old skates to use. I got creative and used empty cans and lids to add to my creations.

I don't remember my Dad being very handy with tools, but we always had a hammer, nails, pliers and screwdrivers. I used them more than he did and he encouraged me to learn! My favorite magazine was Popular Mechanics and I still read any I can find. I was not a good student, but I never failed in school. I was good at wood and metal shop though.

I worked in construction before going into the Army and picked up skills that I didn't have. I learned how to finish concrete, hang and cut sheetrock and do general carpentry.

After my Military service, I went to San Jose Community College and learned Machine Technology, Welding and took all of the required classes. I operated every machine I was exposed to using blueprints and precision measuring tools.

The most important lesson in my trade was safety. If you don't use a machine safely, you can get seriously injured or worse. I met many Machinists with missing fingers.

I still have a love affair with tools. I have woodworking tools that I have accumulated over the years. I like to build furniture and the smell of wood when I am cutting pieces for my projects. I enjoy seeing the end tables and bookcases that I have made. It gives me a sense of accomplishment to see the end result.

When I was working in my trade, I did the same with metal. I took pride in my work. I loved what I was doing, creating things out of metal using all the machines at my disposal with accuracy.

The industry has changed. Work is now done by computer assisted machines or robotics. I embrace change and progress, but I am thankful for the skills I have learned. And to think, it all started with a set of Lincoln Logs and curiosity!

Chapter 25
That's Not How I Remember It

I BELIEVE MEMORIES ARE SNAPSHOTS of your life experiences. Some of the clarity fades with time and your memories depend on your brain, genes, age and how well you took care of your body.

I worked for General Electric at the Motor Plant in San Jose, California for 16 years. I had a good career with the company and it was a great place to work. The wages were good and there were opportunities for advancement.

The Motor Plant was one of the first industrial manufacturing plants in San Jose. It was located in an industrial area at the corner of First Street and Curtner Avenue. In the 70's it employed up to 450 workers and we made a variety of vertical pump motors that ranged from 15 hp to 1500 hp. General Electric also opened a Nuclear Equipment Division Plant a few years later at the same location. It covered almost a square block in area and added more workers and activities to the site.

I was offered a job by PG&E here on the Central Coast with higher pay. My wife Kathy grew up in Arroyo Grande and she encouraged me to take the offer. I pondered my options and thought about where I wanted to live in retirement. I made my choice to leave Silicon Valley and the traffic behind. I had many doubts about my decision but I told myself to do it and not look back.

I left the Motor Plant, my seniority and many friends who didn't think it was a wise decision. But, I said what the hell! I was looking for a job in 1964 when I went to work for General Electric, worked there until 1981 and could look for a job again if it didn't work out with PG&E.

General Electric closed the Motor Plant in San Jose in 1985 and moved their motor manufacturing to Hendersonville, Tennessee and Schenectady, New York. All my old friends thought I was a genius then and that I had some insider knowledge about the plant closure, but it was just luck.

When I go back to the Bay Area, I sometimes pass by the Motor Plant. The only thing that remains on the site is the Motor Plant Administration Building which was preserved for historical reasons. The rest of the site is now a big shopping mall and that is definitely not how I remember it!

I am still nostalgic about the Motor Plant because that is where I was working when I met my wife Kathy and adopted my daughter Maria. Over the years many of my coworkers have passed away and faced serious illnesses, but I still like to remember them as they were when we worked together, the good times we had and the friendships we shared.

Chapter 26
When a Door Opens and Lets the Future In

THE FUTURE IS PART LUCK and part how you deal with your situation. You can either go with the flow or status quo, or you can choose to go in a different direction.

In a Hispanic family, your family is number one. You can choose your friends, but you don't choose your family. You accept them as they are. Human Beings are clannish for the most part.

In the early 1940's most of my relatives were poor and worked wherever they were allowed. We were the last hired and first to be fired except for the work no one else would do. Our education was substandard and if you couldn't speak English you were looked down upon. Most Hispanics who did not speak English were put in the slow classes. Life in the barrio was a vicious circle. If your family stayed there, they all lived by the barrio standards.

I was lucky to have a father that rose above that life. His motto was "I'm no better than anyone, but I'm just as good as anyone." He opened a door to my future by using that criteria. We moved from the barrio and assimilated with the general public. I was lucky to be bilingual all of my life with English as my first language. I'm proud of my heritage and I like speaking Spanish. It has helped in countries where we have traveled.

By using my father's and mother's values to work hard and not be afraid to speak your mind, opportunities opened up for me. Going to college was a pipe dream for someone like me, but "blue collar" work was my ticket to the future. I eventually was able to make more money than some college graduates.

I passed those values to my children and they have done well too. My grandchildren has followed our values also.

I was also able to open a door for someone else. When my sons were going to school, they would bring friends to our home. One boy, Robert, came from a very dysfunctional family. He was the oldest of five children. Both of his parents were alcoholics and he was charged with taking care of his siblings. He was a good friend of all of my sons and we met him when he was in Junior High School. After High School graduation, he asked me if they were hiring where I worked at General Electric in San Jose. I was able to get him an entry level job and I told him if he applied himself he would be able to advance. He followed my advice and rose to Electrical Technician. General Electric closed the plant in 1985 and moved all of the San Jose operations to New York. During this time, Robert married my sister. I was able to get him a job where I currently worked at PG&E in Avila Beach. He just retired after 32 years of service as an Electrical Technician. I guess I opened a couple of doors for him and he never let me down.

I have been fortunate in my life and my family has always been there for me and me for them. I believe in humility. I don't like to sound like I'm bragging about my life or my family. But, I have been blessed in my life and by the doors that have been opened for me. I now have one last door that will be closing in my life in the near future. It has been a good ride.

Chapter 27
Animals I Have Known

THIS IS A GREAT SUBJECT for someone who loves animals. My wife and I can expound on that. We have two animals at present.

Our dog Rusty was rescued from San Luis Obispo County Animal Regulation. Rusty is a six year old Queensland Heeler (Australian Cattle Dog) and German Shepard mix who weighs about sixty pounds. He is a deep red color with freckles on his nose, a white chest and almost looks like a big fox. He has great qualities and is very trainable. He doesn't bark unless someone comes to the door. He likes people and other dogs and is not aggressive. He is loyal, stays close to us, and stays in our yard. He goes and gets the paper every morning before he gets fed. My wife and I are his pack.

We lucked out twice with our last two dogs who were rescues from Animal Regulation. Molly was our previous dog and was the star of the family. She was a mixed breed also, part Border Collie, Australian Shepard and Golden Retriever. She could do everything Rusty does but with much more enthusiasm. We lost her about five years ago, and she left a big hole in our hearts. She loved to ride in the car and traveled with us through half of the United States. She loved my wife, but she was definitely my dog.

Molly is the only dog we have had who would watch TV. She recognized the theme songs from her favorite programs and would come running when she heard them. She also responded to commercial jingles and knew the ones with animals in them. Her favorite programs were America's Funniest Home Videos, Cesar Millan and other animal programs on Animal Planet. When her programs came on, she would run to the TV, circle 360 degrees, run half way down the hall, turn around, then run back and sit in front of the TV. We called that her dance, and she did it every single time!

We had Molly for 13 years. She was a healthy dog, until one night when she woke us up crying and couldn't use her back legs. The Emergency Vet said that she had a tumor that had burst inside her and she had internal bleeding. We had to put her down, one of our saddest days.

My wife has a horse named Rudy that she rides in dressage competitions. He is a 20-year-old off-the-track thoroughbred. We board him on 40 acres behind Lopez Lake. She devotes many hours to riding, grooming and practicing for her competitions. She has been riding since she was nine years old and has owned several horses.

Rusty loves to go to the barn with my wife. He gets to play with his best friend, a boxer named Monkey, but he always keeps an eye on Kathy. He stays close to her when she is at the barn and goes with her when she is riding in the arena or on the trail.

Animals add so much to your life. I can't picture living without them.

Chapter 28
Influenced By

LITERATURE WAS NOT AVAILABLE to me growing up. My parents were both literate in English, but libraries were not accessible. Most were not in our neighborhoods and we had no books at home. Our stories were told by the adults as folklore. Later the radio opened up the world to me.

We read in school about Dick, Jane, Spot and Baby Sally. I couldn't relate to that family because it was so different from our family. As an adult, I have read novels by John Steinbeck such as the *Grapes of Wrath*, *East of Eden*, and *The Pearl*. I can relate to their lives because we lived in very similar conditions.

Movies were my favorite pastime. I liked movies with Hispanics like Anthony Quinn, Rita Hayworth and Martin Sheen. Many of them had to change their names to work in the movie industry.

One of my favorite movies was *The Days of Wine*

and Roses. It made me understand alcoholism and its impact on families. Being of Indian decent, we had several uncles that were winos, the term used to describe them in those days. Most of them left their families and jobs because of their alcohol addiction.

My Father was not very tolerant of his older brothers who suffered from that disease. He labeled them lazy and wouldn't help them. My Mother, however, always fed them and gave them money. My Father did his share of drinking on Friday nights and Saturday. Drinking was thought of as an adult recreation in my culture.

The movie was powerful in it's content and the music was great! I remember the year was 1962 because another favorite movie of mine, To Kill A Mockingbird, also came out the same year. This movie struck a chord with me because a black man was falsely accused of a crime. It also showed the courage it took for a white lawyer to take his case, the impact it had on his life and the mood of the south during the Depression. I also read and liked the book by Harper Lee.

Another movie I can relate to and really liked is My Family which came out in 1995. The families in the story resembled our family and our problems, plus they looked like us.

As an 82-year-old with a fairly good memory, music is my narcotic of choice. I like most kinds of music, but especially the music of the 50's, 60's, 70's and 80's. Most of the time I can remember who made it famous. That is why I attend Concerts in the Park in our community and don't mind paying to watch it if tickets are under $50. We have a lot of great musicians in the area, and my wife Kathy and I support the Arts in our area.

I spend a lot of time now enjoying a good book and visit the library often. I wish I would have discovered books at an earlier age. But, it's never too late to discover new pleasure, even at my age.

Chapter 29
*Famous Last Words
(You're Not Going to Make It)*

WHEN MY GRANDSON JEFFERY graduated from High School, he told his father that was was going to enlist in the Navy and become a Navy Seal. My son asked me to give him my advice on his decision and he came to visit us to talk about this. Being ex-military, I gave him my opinion on the matter. I told him the Navy Recruiters will promise you anything to get you to sign up so they could meet their quotas. I suggested he look at the statistics regarding how many recruits apply and how many graduate as a Navy Seal. I told him "You are not going to make it, it's too tough."

His father and I suggested he join the Air Force instead to minimize the risk of combat and being in harms way. He respectfully took our advice and enlisted in the Air Force.

After completion of Basic Training at Lackland Air Force Base, we flew to San Antonio, Texas for his graduation ceremony. He told us he was going to be stationed at McCord Air Force Base in Washington State. We were all happy he would be on the West Coast.

Jeff failed to tell us he had chosen and been accepted as part of the a Special Forces Unit, the Air Force's branch similar to the Navy Seals. In fact, he trained with the Seals in San Diego. He went to Jump School at Fort Bragg, North Carolina, did desert training in California, and extensive training in Washington with the Army Rangers.

His job was to go into remote areas in Afghanistan with other Special Forces units like the British Commandos, the Danish Rangers, and the US Army Pathfinders, also known as the Green Berets. They went in by helicopters, and he would find the location and be the first on the ground to establish and secure the area. He called for air support if needed and to have the wounded evacuated. He was deployed four times to Afghanistan and was wounded once. He came back suffering from PTSD.

Jeff was decorated with the Bronze Star, one with Valor, for three out of the four deployments. He served eight years in the Air Force, and we were proud of him, but concerned. He was dealing with depression and PTSD. We had long talks about his service and our concerns for his survival. We convinced him not to re-enlist and assured him he had done more than his duty for his country.

He re-entered civilian life and went through counseling. He doesn't get depressed as often. He enrolled in the University of Washington through the GI Bill. He is doing great in school and loves his classes. He calls me often, and we have a great relationship. His wife is a sweetheart who stood by him through the difficult times, and they are a great, supportive couple.

The military will use you as much as you let them but they will replace you like a flat tire when they are done. The VA is more responsive these days than they were in my day when finding VA help was like finding a needle in a haystack. My grandson is getting the benefits he deserves, and I'm happy for him.

Sometimes you have have to eat your misspoken words! Jeff proved us wrong when we told him, "You are not going to make it!

Chapter 30
What Do You Want to Be When You Grow Up?

THIS IS AN INTERESTING QUESTION. It is one that can only be answered as your life experience allows and by the choices you make.

My childhood dreams were the same as most children but with limited options. The saying "You can grow up and be anything you want" did not apply to a Hispanic child in the 1940's and 1950's. There was a very short ladder to reach your goals. You had to know your place in that society. We encountered signs such as "Mexicans need not apply" or "That position has already been filled." I use to dream about being a pilot but I knew it was an impossible dream.

I liked to build things as a child with 2x4s, orange crates, nails and empty tin cans. I kept that as my focus and after my military service I asked myself "Why not me?" and expected an answer. I became more assertive and used my Father's analogy "I am no better than anyone, but I'm just as good as anyone." Doors started opening for me. I took advantage of the opportunities and went to Community College to learn my trade. I could make anything out of metal from a blueprint. I also used my ability communicate and get along with those around me. I consider myself successful in my working life. I made good money and was able to save much of it for my retirement.

I think I was lucky and there were a lot more employment opportunities in the late 1950's and 1960's. I worked until I was 80 years old and I declined offers to go back after that.

I was able to fulfill one of my childhood dreams as an adult. I got my Private Pilot's License in the early 1970's and flew until health issues made me give it up.

My biggest accomplishment is my family. My wife Kathy deserves a lot of credit for that. I feel my family has succeeded in their lives. I still don't know how to measure success, but I feel blessed. I reflect back on those early years, the lessons learned, and I feel good about myself.

I believe if life gives you lemons, make lemonade and things will turn out alright. Now in my declining years, I still try to be the best I can be and treat people with respect and kindness.

There is an old saying "The only good thing about the good old days is that they are gone." I disagree because they taught me good lessons and values that are not used today. I have learned over the years not to be envious of what others have. Even if my life turned out different than I dreamed it would as a child, I am very thankful for how it turned out.

Chapter 31
A Year of Aging

THE YEAR 2017 HAS NOT BEEN MY BEST YEAR. As I reach the autumn of my life, I have many different feelings that are new and confusing.

My physical condition is greatly diminishing. It takes me twice as long to do half as much as I use to do. I understand that your body slows down, and you are not as flexible as you once were, but your mind has to understand that you can't do what you were able to routinely do in the past.

I don't hear well and I have to ask people to repeat themselves. I don't think I am ready for a hearing aid yet, but some might disagree. I also have a tremor in my right hand which is getting worse. I have recently been diagnosed with the first stages of Parkinson's disease. It affects my guitar playing and wood working skills. I do get depressed dealing with my limitations. Although I can face these problems, I don't want to be a burden to my family and drain them emotionally or financially.

I come from a different era. Family was always close to where we lived. The elderly were valued for their wisdom and experience. They were never sent away to be warehoused in a rest home. Life expectancy was shorter, and they passed in a family member's home. How times have changed. Now family members live far away and you seldom see your grandchildren or great-grandchildren unless it is on Facebook or Skype. I miss taking them for walks or ice cream. I miss the old days.

I was trained to work with my hands and taught how to use tools. I wish I could pass those skills to my family members, but they are scattered all over the country. I would love to babysit my grandchildren and great-grandchildren to help their parents with daycare expenses.

I guess I live in the past. Have we really evolved? What do I know? I am just a relic from the past.

I am amazed at the technology age with computers, iPads and iPhones. All of my family is well supplied with the latest and greatest devices. However, I appreciate when they look up from their cell phones. They discover I have something to contribute too! I believe in using those devices, but with respect to those around you. I prefer engaging in a conversation and looking into their eyes. I appreciate their phone calls and greeting cards, which is all I expect at this stage of my life. I have everything I need. Life is good and I have lived well, better than I feel I deserve.

I believe if you do everything with a good heart and expect nothing return you will never be disappointed.

Chapter 32
Where Would You Like to Go This Year? Who Would You Like to Go With?

THERE ARE TWO TRIPS I would like to take this year. The first is to Portugal and Spain in October. It is my wife's birth month and and since it is a milestone birthday, she gets to choose where she wants to go. She has suggested Spain and Portugal which is fine with me. I have always wanted to go to both countries. My wife is the person I like to travel with most. We plan our trips together and are pretty compatible travelers. We have occasionally had our moments when things didn't go as planned, but nothing is perfect.

We also have our own separate interests. My wife has a horse (Rudy) and rides English style. She competes in dressage shows as an amateur. I like to play golf with a group of friends. We travel to Nevada and Palm Springs for tournaments. Although my golf game is going south, I have enjoyed all the years I have played, the places I have traveled to and the people I met along the way.

Another trip I would like to take this year is to retrace my past. My youngest son, who turns 60 this year, wants to revisit Southern California with me. I lived in the LA area from 1935 to 1944, before we moved to the Santa Clara Valley. I still remember the streets we lived on and the different neighborhoods. My Mother lived in East LA until the riots in the late 1960's. The neighborhoods had gotten very dangerous, so we sold her house and she moved to San Jose with my sister.

My youngest son spent many summers with his grandma and my sister when they lived in East LA. He wants to go back with me to revisit those places and help me fulfill an item that is on my bucket list. The years are passing quickly and my time is getting shorter. Over the years the friends I have known have drifted away and I am the only one left to see how the neighborhoods have wasted away.

I expect to find big changes. My memories are of a simpler time when you knew most of your neighbors and people talked to each other. I guess I shouldn't dwell on the past and try to embrace the present, but it's hard for an old relic like me!

Chapter 33
Road Scholar

KATHY AND I BOTH LIKE TO TRAVEL. We have problems making travel choices sometimes but alway compromise on our decision.

I have always been curious about Cuba, and I like the music. Relations between Cuba and the US were improving, and I wanted to see it before the embargo was lifted and there was a McDonalds or Starbucks on every corner.

Two years ago we decided to travel there. The US is very strict about who is allowed to travel to Cuba. You have to go with certain cultural organizations or groups. We chose a people-to-people tour with Road Scholar. They were a terrific group to travel with and took care of all the arrangements so we could travel to Cuba and meet the US guidelines.

We all met in Miami. My wife and I arrived a week early so we could take a road trip to the Florida Keys and the Everglades. We met our tour group at a hotel in Miami and flew to Cienfuegos, Cuba. We stayed in their best hotel. All of our meals and lodging were handled by Road Scholar. We had a bilingual Cuban guide and our own tour leader with us for the trip. Both were excellent. Our Cuban guide spoke fluent English, gave us all the history and would answer all of our questions. We were a group of about 24 people, mostly Americans. We traveled in a new Chinese Bus which was similar to any seen in the US.

Cuba itself reminded me of the 50's. Not only were the cars familiar but the buildings, houses and modes of transport looked like they were in a time warp. The people were very friendly and respectful. There was no begging or trying to sell you things like we had experienced in other Latin American countries, which was refreshing.

Every day we were taken to a cultural site to visit. Our first stop was at the Benny More Musical Academy, one of the most prestigious music schools in the country. Each year, two to three thousand students apply but only about a hundred are accepted. They performed for us and we were all very impressed. We were encouraged to bring items to donate, and I brought forty sets of guitar strings for them. I was also impressed that Cuba has a 99% literacy rate. The students were very respectful to their guests.

We traveled to Trinidad and Santa Clara before we headed to Havana. Santa Clara has a Monument for Che Gueverra. Along the way we went to a Museum for the Bay of Pigs, a source of pride for the Cubans. They don't talk much about communism.

Public transportation is non-existent in Cuba. Instead, people wait by the side of the road for a ride. Cubans are required to stop for those needing a ride. There are Traffic Observers that will report anyone who doesn't stop to pick up riders including horse drawn carts or trucks without benches in the back.

There isn't a lot of traffic on the roads outside of the cities, so the farmers make good use of the tarmac of the road to dry rice.

As we arrived in Havana, we saw many historical buildings that needed a lot of restoration. They could sure use a Home Depot! We toured an art gallery and visited the only English bookstore in Havana. It was run by an American woman and staffed with young English speaking university students who were anxious to engage us in conversation.

We stayed in the best hotel in Havana. We were wined and dined at the better restaurants. Everything was handled by our tour guide, including tipping.

One afternoon we were scheduled to go to a nice restaurant. We gathered in the hotel lobby but were told our bus had broken down. We were all disappointed and trying to figure out how we would get to the restaurant. All of a sudden, a line of 1950 convertible cars drove up. They were there to take our group to the restaurant! We hit the road. We drove through the best neighborhoods of Havana and took lots of pictures of us in the cars. After we finished dinner and had a great group sing and dance for us, our bus was waiting to take us back to the hotel. It had not broken down at all. The evening turned out to be the highlight of our trip.

The people of Cuba were very nice. They like Americans, but don't like our government. Of course, we don't like theirs, either. We learned a lot during our trip. The government pays everyone $20 per month, but they have to work for the money. The embargo has really hurt Cuba. Russia was a big trading partner until they left a big void when they pulled out of Cuba on July 3, 1993. I guess Russia had big problems of their own. In retrospect, the Cuban communist experience failed, but they kept their focus on education and the arts. To fill the void, Cuba exports teachers, doctors, and other professional people to other countries in

Latin America along with cigars, rum and coffee. We brought home Cuban cigars and coffee to enjoy. Cuba is fifty years behind the rest of the world.

Our group was a 50-and-over bunch from all over the country, and we all seemed to get along. We still keep in contact with a few of them. It turned out to be a great trip that we enjoyed immensely. But, it is always great to get back to our home country.

Chapter 34
What Was I Thinking?

MY INTENTIONS WITH THESE PAGES are to leave you a testimony of my life. I hope you might stop and remember me some day when you are less busy.

Now that I am at the advanced age of 88, I feel the impact of my age and living with Parkinson's. Both have taken their toll. I feel blessed to have lived in this era. Having been born at the end of the Great Depression, I knew how poor we were. Like everyone else, we sacrificed for the war effort during World War II. I came of age in the 1950s during the Korean War years and lived through the Vietnam war in the turbulent 1960s. I learned discipline, how to be a good soldier, how to get along with others and how to supervise those who I was responsible for during my service in the Korean War.

After my Tour of Duty, I returned home to my wife Carmen and my three sons. I worked hard to support my family and purchase our first home. I enrolled in Night School to get my High School diploma and went to college to earn a degree as a Machine Technician. This served me well until retirement.

Looking back at my life, I have no regrets and tried to make the most of opportunities offered to me. I have learned to be grateful for what I have and not envy others. I enjoy looking back at the early years and especially the summers at Bass Lake with all my family members who chose to come.

To my grandchildren, I'm sorry I didn't know you as well as I could have, but there were too many miles between us.

I am fortunate to have my sister Pat close by who is always looking out for me. I love her very much!

I am blessed to have my wife Kathy, who I love the most, for 44 years of happy marriage.

Special thanks to my grandson Jeff for encouraging me to take pen to paper to tell my story.

Just know that family matters most!

Ernie Salazar

Afterword
From Sierras to Salazar and Beyond

WHERE DID THE *SALAZAR* NAME come from? More importantly, who blessed this family with it? While it is nearly impossible to answer these questions in their entirety, as *Salazar* is considered a fairly common name among Spanish-speaking communities, a trail of evidence exists that can help track its evolution into a single family unit.

The origins of the surname *Salazar* can be traced to Spain as *the dweller in, or near, the house or palace; dweller near the place sacred to St. Lazar*. From Latin we find the root as *salis*, a place for salting fish and meat, with nearly ninety ancient surnames found in Vizcaya, Castile, Navarre, Santander, and so on. It is the name of a village in Burgos that dates from the period of Charlemagne, which itself is derived from a Basque word meaning *palicio*.[1]

---

[1] R. D. Woods and G. Alvarez-Altman, *Spanish Surnames in the Southwestern United States A Dictionary* (Boston: G.K. Hall, 1978).

Alternatively, the name *Sierras* has its own history as well, deeply entrenched in the American narrative. Confronted with the realities of colonization, the Southwestern United States has a long and troubled history with Spanish interference. As the Indigenous communities surrounding the Tucson, Arizona area (Pima, Papago, Maricopa, Mayo, etc.) were driven out of their ancestral lands and forced into what colonists viewed as "civilization" a rush to label occurred. People stemming from tribal lands were given names based on where they came from, and *Sierras* is just one of many that applied to this situation. Roughly translating to *dweller among saw-shaped mountains*, or, one who comes from Sierra (saw-toothed mountain), someone who lives near or around mountains.

Specifically speaking, the Pima communities were *people of the river*, yet their communal lived areas were much more broad than that and were divided into subgroups by the Spanish clergy as either people of the mountains (i.e. Sierras) or people of the river (i.e. Rios). Thus, families were then organized a diluted into the laborers that colonists needed to run their farms.

How is it, then, that the Sierras family came to be disconnected and removed from our ancestral lands, "lost ones" from the community we've been attached to since time immemorial? The painful answer distills down to a single word: *water*. The Colorado River is a powerful source of life. Stretching for hundreds of miles and feeding lands with countless tributaries and run-offs that sustain verdant lifescapes. However, 200-years of theft by law and redistribution by non-Indigenous politicians have starved communities and literally choked entire landscapes. The Gila River was one of the many water sources diverted away from Indigenous communities feeding the Akimel O'odham (Pima) and the Pee-Posh (Maricopa) tribes and effectively drove many away from their lands.

Juan Tomás Sierras, born sometime in 1887 in or around the area of Tucson, Arizona, was directly affected by these policies of diversion. No records exist of his place of birth, but his activity suggests an outward movement from that area—coinciding with a deadly famine that gripped his community until 1904. He was the fourth son of eight children from the union of *Gregoria Ortiz* (b. 1858) and *Braulio Sierras*. Unable to continue the ancestral practice of farming and land husbandry he, along with so many others, turned to the hard labor being asked of the very people who benefited from the water siphoned away from their communities. Thus, Juan Sierras began his employment with the historic Empire Ranch and quickly became an indispensable asset to their operation. Known for his hard work, reliability, and tenacity, Juan is an integral part of their history and has been recognized as such. As the ranch grew and expanded their operations to California, Juan was one of the first workers sent to work the future fields of operation.

Functionally unable to revive his community and facing an overwhelming power dynamic he did the only things he felt he could do—leave. Thus, a throughline emerges as to the origin, migration, and disconnection of our family from our ancestral community. Juan's success at his work allowed him to grow his family. The widespread progeny of Juan Tomás Sierras resulted in a family tree that is truly vast and encourages a redefinition of extended family. One direct branch of that family tree involved his first recorded spouse: *Dolores Estrada (Salazar)*, and it is these parentheses that we should focus on. Their union produced *Ernesto Sierras (Salazar)* and to hear Ernesto say it, in his own words:

> When they met, she was already married to a man named *Salazar*, which she had four kids with him already. When my father [Ernesto] was born, Juan took off, and he never knew him. Juan and Dolores's relationship was more of a casual one. He was raised

in a house where all his brothers had the name Salazar, and he didn't want to be different. Since he never knew his dad, he took Salazar as his name. He didn't meet his dad until he was fifteen. He didn't know him, and Sierras didn't mean anything to him.

After Juan left Dolores he married twice more and fathered sixteen children, all of whom remained relatively unknown to Ernesto for many years. However, after a series of reunions and gatherings, he now enjoys the company of many of them and sees them as often as he can.

While it may seem tempting to some to place a modern critique on the decisions made in the past, I would caution those who wish to do so. We need to remember that in the vast space of time between then and now, the sociality of norms also flexed as generations marched forward to today. I've done my best to gather as much surviving information as possible, but these few sentences do not do justice to the complicated, nuanced, and diverse lives that made us who we are. What does survive, though, is a continuous line of love—unbroken in its truth and amazing in its multiplicity. *Ernesto Montellano Salazar, Jr.* continues this tradition and is surrounded by a family burgeoning with love for him, the man who made this all possible. *–Jeff Salazar*

www.ingramcontent.com/pod-product-compliance
Lightning Source LLC
Chambersburg PA
CBHW070115080526
44586CB00013B/1300